JE 1 7

12 GREAT TIPS ON
WRITING A SCRIPT

by Barbara Krasner

12 STORY LIBRARY

www.12StoryLibrary.com

12-Story Library is an imprint of Peterson Publishing Company and Press Room Editions.

Produced for 12-Story Library by Red Line Editorial

Photographs ©: Jupiterimages/Thinkstock, cover, 1; g-stockstudio/iStockphoto, 4; YinYang/iStockphoto, 5; Minerva Studio/Shutterstock Images, 6; AP Images, 7; alphaspirit/iStock/Thinkstock, 8, 28; Library of Congress, 9; Eldad Yitzhak/Shutterstock Images, 10; skodonnell/iStockphoto, 11; ferrantraite/iStockphoto, 12; Pavel L Photo and Video/Shutterstock Images, 14; Igor Bulgarin/Shutterstock Images, 15, 17, 22, 29; wrangel/iStockphoto, 16; NDT/Shutterstock Images, 18; Steve Debenport/iStockphoto, 20; Christian Bertrand/Shutterstock Images, 23; Monkey Business Images/Shutterstock Images, 24; bikeriderlondon/Shutterstock Images, 25; seandeburca/iStockphoto, 26; karamysh/Shutterstock Images, 27

Library of Congress Cataloging-in-Publication Data
Names: Krasner, Barbara.
Title: 12 great tips on writing a script / by Barbara Krasner.
Other titles: Twelve great tips on writing a script
Description: Mankato, MN : 12-Story Library, 2017. | Series: Great tips on
   writing | Includes bibliographical references and index.
Identifiers: LCCN 2016002324 (print) | LCCN 2016005707 (ebook) | ISBN
   9781632352767 (library bound : alk. paper) | ISBN 9781632353269 (pbk. :
   alk. paper) | ISBN 9781621434443 (hosted ebook)
Subjects: LCSH: Playwriting--Juvenile literature. | Motion picture
   authorship--Juvenile literature. | Television authorship--Juvenile
   literature.
Classification: LCC PN1661 .K64 2016 (print) | LCC PN1661 (ebook) | DDC
   808.2--dc23
LC record available at http://lccn.loc.gov/2016002324

Printed in the United States of America
Mankato, MN
May, 2016

Access free, up-to-date content on this topic plus a full digital version of this book. Scan the QR code on page 31 or use your school's login at 12StoryLibrary.com.

Table of Contents

Write What Interests You

You've decided to write a script for stage, screen, or television. Congratulations! You have an exciting journey ahead of you. Your first step toward creating that script is to come up with an idea.

Asking "what if" is a powerful way to come up with new ideas. For example, what if the sun didn't come up one morning? What if your clothes were suddenly too big or too small?

Reading can help you get ideas.

Or you might already have things you want to write about. Perhaps you have had a vivid dream that has stuck with you. Or maybe you want to write about a book or an item in a magazine or newspaper. You might admire a family member or friend and want to write about that person.

Quick Tips

- Generate lots of ideas.
- Narrow them down to those that give you energy.
- Choose one you can see on the stage or screen.

THINK ABOUT IT

Pull out your list of possible story ideas. Which one could you actually see on a stage or screen? Choose one you can visualize the best.

You could also brainstorm some ideas. Give yourself a time limit, say 10 minutes, and make a list of ideas.

Not all the ideas you come up with will work well on stage or screen. You need to find out which story you are most interested in, which story gives you the most energy. Review your list and monitor your own reaction to the ideas. Do some make your heart beat a little faster? Put a star next to those.

Your ultimate goal is to write a story that keeps your audience interested. You want your audience to relate to your story emotionally. That means you must, too.

Let's say you've chosen the idea for your script. Let it sit for a day, a week, or even a month. Now come back to it. Does it still excite you? Now you know you've chosen well.

It may take many tries to find the right idea.

Plan Out
Your Story

Expert screenwriters say that planning to write takes up about 65 percent of the time to create a screenplay. Leading playwrights, for example, thoroughly outline their stories before actually writing their scripts.

What's involved in planning? First, you need to think about what happens in your story. This is called the plot. You probably have a main character in mind who serves as your hero. That character has to have a problem and has to face challenges to get what he or she wants. Think about the movie *The Wizard of Oz*. After a twister hits her home, Dorothy finds herself in a new land where everything is strange. She wants to go home. That sets up the plot for her journey, where she

Characters can face challenges from other people or from nature.

is tested by the Wicked Witch of the West before she can return home.

For now, sketch out what you think your story will be. Draw pictures of what you think important moments in each scene will look like. A scene has a beginning, a middle, and an end. It takes place in a certain place and time. If you move the action to another place or another time, then you need a new scene. Scenes are your building blocks. They come together to form the story structure.

Glinda the Good Witch (left) helps Dorothy on her journey back to Kansas.

3

Choose a Hero and Establish a Goal

Every play and movie presents a leading character—a hero. Most often, the hero wants to achieve something. It could be wealth. It could be fame. It could be love. In *The Wizard of Oz,* Dorothy is the hero. Her goal is to return home to Kansas.

Who should your hero be? You should choose a character your audience can relate to. If you want to write a play for school, your hero could be a student, teacher, or school staff member. What does your hero like to do? What does he or she not like to do? How well does your hero get along with others at school? At home? You want to give your audience a hero they want to spend time with, someone they could care about.

What kind of goal should you give your hero?

Heroes do not need to be superheroes, but they can be.

Think of something that tests your hero. The goal should be difficult to achieve but not impossible. Maybe she wants to win the basketball championship. Maybe he's a foster child and wants a permanent home. Look for a specific, positive goal.

The Tin Man is one of Dorothy's companions during her quest.

The plot centers on your hero's attempts to attain the goal. But the hero does not need to be alone. Secondary characters can help your hero overcome challenges. These characters might include trusted friends, parents, teachers, brothers, or sisters. In *The Wizard of Oz*, Dorothy has the Tin Man, the Cowardly Lion, and the Scarecrow who help. Glinda, the Good Witch of the North, also helps Dorothy defeat the Wicked Witch.

FRED R. HAMLIN'S MUSICAL EXTRAVAGANZ

THE WIZARD OF OZ

• THE TIN MAN •

Quick Tips

- Select one of your characters as your hero.
- Make your hero relatable to your audience.
- Give your hero a positive goal to pursue.

TRY IT OUT

Name your hero. Write down three possible goals for this character. Who are your secondary characters? What do they want to achieve?

4

Use
Three Acts

Every story has a beginning, a middle, and an end. That gives you a three-act structure: Act One, Act Two, and Act Three.

Act One is the beginning and sets up the story. It introduces the audience to the characters. Some incident, usually placed toward the end of the first act, puts the plot in motion, such as the twister in *The Wizard of Oz*.

Act Two is the middle, where your character gets tested and it looks like your hero will never achieve what he or she wants. The villain seems to have the upper hand, and all hope seems to be lost. In Act Two of *The Wizard of Oz*, the Wicked Witch captures Dorothy.

The hero usually faces very difficult situations in Act Two.

BEGINNING, MIDDLE, AND END

Act One: Andrew and Devon learn a secret about Mrs. Alcott, a young teacher who always seems to be followed by a black cat. They think she's a witch. They decide to spy on her.

Act Two: Andrew falls headfirst into a trash bin while trying to observe Mrs. Alcott's actions. Devon slips on a banana peel when following Mrs. Alcott outside the school. Andrew and Devon find her with a box of black kittens.

Act Three: Andrew and Devon learn Mrs. Alcott cares for homeless animals. They apologize for their mistake and they volunteer to help, too.

Act Three is the end. Your hero and villain face off. The conflict is resolved. Good Witch Glinda tells Dorothy she has always had the power to go home and the Wicked Witch melts. Clicking the heels of her red shoes, Dorothy returns home to her loving family.

Some writers tweak or elaborate on the three-act structure. But it is

Quick Tips

- Use the power of three—three acts.
- Develop a clear beginning, middle, and end.
- Include a point where your hero loses hope.
- Include a point where your hero faces the opposition.

the most common way to write a script. Using three acts will help you organize your thoughts—and your scenes.

Dorothy wore magical ruby red slippers that helped her get home.

5

See It, Write It

A movie or play must create pictures in a viewer's mind. That means you should see pictures, too, in your mind's eye as you write. You must translate what you see using visual language.

That's why scripts have special formatting. They clearly identify the character speaking and include gestures or actions the characters take. This helps the producer, director, and the actors bring your script to life on stage or screen.

To begin writing your screenplay, start by describing the exterior shot, for example, the way a camera should picture a building in downtown Los Angeles. Then identify where your actors are. Describe what they are doing. This is your scene heading. Now you're

Actors memorize scripts so they can act them out.

FORMATTING A SCRIPT

Scriptwriting requires a certain format for writing scene headings, scene directions, and dialogue:

EXTERIOR: HAMILTON ELEMENTARY SCHOOL, 8:45 AM

INTERIOR: OUTSIDE MRS. ALCOTT'S ROOM, 32

ANDREW and DEVON stand in front of their classroom.

ANDREW

I knew it would end up like this.

(sound of footsteps)

DEVON

Quick! Here she comes!

(Enter MRS. ALCOTT. She is followed by a black cat.)

ready to move to the dialogue. Center the character's name on the page. Then write the dialogue below it. Using parentheses, be sure to include any gestures the character makes. This will tell the actor what to do on the stage or set. It is called the scene direction for a screenplay and stage direction for a theatrical play.

Other things to think about in the formatting of your script are sound effects. Should a phone be ringing during your scene? Is music playing? For TV or movies, you need to think about camera angles, too—long shot, medium shot, or close up.

There's a lot to think about! But don't worry. If you can see your story playing out in your mind's eye, you can put it to paper.

Quick Tips

- See your story in your mind's eye as your write.
- Think about how the actors should move around on the set or stage.
- Consider sound effects and camera angles.

13

Keep Your Audience in Mind

Your script needs more than just plot and characters to keep your audience in their seats. You need to make your story come alive. Stage directions, written within parentheses in your script, help you do that. Visualize, for example, how and when your characters will enter or exit a scene. Describe all the actions and gestures your characters make down to the tiniest details. Consider what props they may need. In *The Wizard of Oz,* Dorothy's red slippers are a must. So is the hot air balloon that takes her home. And don't forget about her dog, Toto, and the basket that carries him!

Characters on stage always need to be doing something.

Quick Tips

- Know the audience you want to write for.
- Imagine the set or stage the way your audience will see it.
- Act out your script to make sure you account for gestures and actions.

TRY IT OUT

Describe the type of people you expect to have in your audience. What do they like and dislike? What sort of story do you think they want to see?

A good way to ensure you include the necessary directions in your script is to imagine yourself in the audience. What do you see? Act out what you write. Are you missing any gestures? Have you accounted for every character's entrance and exit for each scene? Do you see opportunities for more props? Fewer props?

Imagine the set or stage the way the audience will see it. Some playwrights build small models of the stage and use stick figures as their characters. Others get up on a real stage and act out their scripts. Doing these things can give you important perspective about your writing.

Using props effectively can greatly improve a scene.

15

Put Obstacles in the Way of Your Hero

To keep your audience interested in your story, you must introduce tension. One method for increasing tension is to keep your hero from easily meeting his or her goals. For example, will the Wicked Witch be Dorothy's doom? Or will Dorothy and her friends be victorious?

Challenges can take many forms. They can be physical, such as a twister. They can be about relationships, for example, the separation of sisters. Villains can present obstacles. For example, the Wicked Witch constantly pursues Dorothy and her red slippers. Culture can create conflict. For instance, Dorothy is not happy living on her aunt and uncle's farm. All of these are examples of outer conflict.

An inner conflict can also present problems. Heroes must decide what to do when obstacles arise. Often these decisions are difficult. Dorothy is

War is an example of physical conflict.

an orphan and she feels like she doesn't belong. But she overcomes the Wicked Witch and her initial fear of the Wizard so she can return to her aunt. The place she doesn't feel is home before the cyclone hit becomes the place she must get back to.

Presenting your hero with obstacles will help prevent your audience from getting bored. They will continue to ask, "What happens next?" Each obstacle you use should be different. Each should be harder to overcome than the one that came before it. Aim for three major problems that set your hero back from achieving his or her goal.

As a result of overcoming challenges, your hero will not be the same person as the one in the opening scene. He or she will have grown as a person after passing tests of increasing difficulty.

Strong emotions can create conflict.

Quick Tips

- Create instances of outer conflict for your hero.
- Create instances of inner conflict for your hero.
- Make sure each obstacle is harder for your hero to overcome than the one that came before it.

TRY IT OUT

Name three obstacles you plan to put in front of your main character. Use both inner and outer conflict. How will these challenge him or her? What will change as a result?

Keep Your Setting Simple

Whether writing a screenplay or a stage play, it is important to build a believable world for your story. It could be a present-day school or a 19th-century plantation during the US Civil War. Actors may need costumes and complex props. Set design may require more staff to accommodate multiple scenes in different locations. You might have special effects in mind. Maybe your script calls for a car chase or an explosion. But take note.

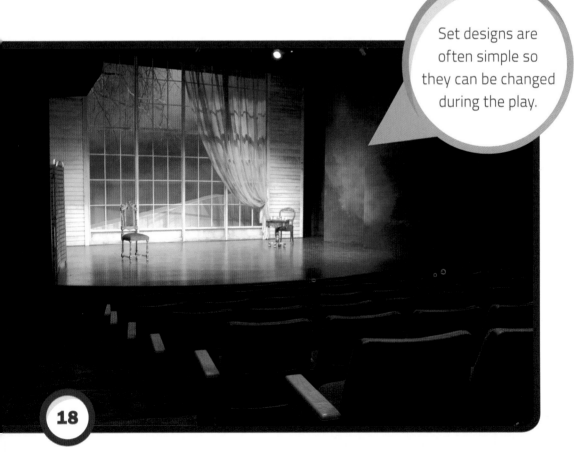

Set designs are often simple so they can be changed during the play.

The more complex a stage setting or film location, the more expensive production can be. Leading writers work hard to use as few props and sets as necessary. They also minimize the number of scenes and scene changes.

Another reason to keep your setting simple is for ease of production. What if your scene requires 10 hand props and only seven make it to the set? If you plan for two, you have a greater chance for success.

If your screenplay requires a change in weather, say, a hurricane, think about ways to show the changes without extra expense. Ask yourself, too, whether you really need a hurricane in your story. Could it take place after a hurricane?

Ultimately, you may want to consider a single location for your script. Characters can enter and exit to keep the plot moving forward.

Quick Tips

- Build a believable world for your story.
- Keep the number of locations to a minimum.
- Keep the number of scene changes to a minimum.
- Consider production ease.

KEEP YOUR SETTING SIMPLE

Setting Element	Simple	Complex
Scene	A living room, today	A spaceship in outer space, the year 2200
Hand props	A book, a cell phone	A communicator, a wall that shows 3-D images
Costumes	Everyday clothing	Space suits made of special rubber material

Make Dialogue Sing

When two or more people talk to one another on stage, it is called dialogue. Dialogue carries more weight in a play or TV screenplay than in other forms of writing. It moves the plot forward. It shows characters' personalities. It reveals information and fills in gaps for the audience. It connects scenes.

But when dialogue is weighed down with unnecessary words, the script drags. Viewers lose interest. To avoid this, say more with less. Think about what you can show rather than tell. If your character is happy, have him do a happy dance or a cartwheel, rather than say in dialogue, "I'm happy." You can have characters finish each other's sentences or cut one another off. Actions such as these make it so the dialogue doesn't need to show every detail.

Make sure your dialogue fits its speaker. Each character should have a distinctive voice. This depends on the character's background. Someone living in New York City will

Good dialogue is essential to a successful script.

SNAPPY DIALOGUE

In a script, dialogue has many responsibilities, such as showing character, giving the audience information, and moving the plot forward.

> ANDREW
> I'm telling you, she's a witch.
> DEVON
> How can you tell?
> ANDREW
> Remember on Halloween? She wore those skeleton earrings?
> DEVON
> Lots of women probably wear those.
> ANDREW
> And those long fingernails?
> DEVON
> My sister has long fingernails. That doesn't mean anything.
> ANDREW
> Oh, no? Do your sister's glow in the dark?

not sound the same as someone from a farm in Iowa. A teenager will not use the same kinds of words as a college professor.

If you were to listen to a conversation, you might hear *um*, *so*, *you know*, and other words and phrases that add little meaning to a sentence. Although we may use them in everyday life, be mindful not to overuse them in your script. Keep the dialogue crisp and flowing. One way to think about dialogue is a Ping-Pong game. It should be short and snappy, back and forth.

Quick Tips

- Show, don't tell.
- Say more with less.
- Keep filler words like *um*, *so*, and *you know* to a minimum.
- Think of dialogue as a game of Ping-Pong.

21

Keep Your Characters Busy

Master writers of stage and screen know how to best use their character's body language for action. They also know how to make full use of the physical space. When they prepare their scripts, they include both small actions, such as sitting on a sofa, and big actions that require the set to be moved around, such as a struggle on stage or a car chase on screen. They make sure everyone in the scene has something to do.

Imagine you've written a party scene for your stage play. Each character in that scene must have something to do. Let's say you have your main character and two secondary characters in the scene. Your

Scenes sometimes have many actors on stage.

- Include physical action in your script.
- Make sure your characters all have an activity to carry out.
- Eliminate characters who have nothing to do.

TRY IT OUT

Review what you've written so far. Does each of your characters have a specific activity? Have you accounted for it in your stage directions?

main character sits on the sofa, standing up each time someone new enters. He's looking for the girl he's invited. She finally enters, and he approaches her with a big teddy bear. They speak. Meanwhile, others in the scene are eating and dancing. That's how the audience knows it's a party.

In your script, you must include stage directions for all characters, including the ensemble, or extras. In *The Wizard of Oz*, Dorothy lands in Munchkinland after the cyclone. The scene includes dozens of little people, called Munchkins. Each of the Munchkins has a task to carry out on the screen. If you do not have enough activity for all your players, you may need to get rid of some.

Actions should be clear and strong. What makes a strong action? It should be a physical action that plants an image in the minds of the viewers.

Movements should be clear and strong so the audience notices them.

11

Revise Your Script

Most writing is actually done during the revision process. Revision means "re-seeing" what you have written.

Reread your script and ask yourself whether you have developed a believable world, a believable plot, believable characters, and a goal for your hero that is worth striving for. Is there enough conflict? Is your hero tested? Ask a few trusted friends or adults to review your work. Their feedback can help you see things that you missed.

One of the best ways to know what you should rewrite is to read your script aloud. This will help you notice when dialogue moves the action too

Having others read your writing can help you see it differently.

Quick Tips

- Ask for feedback from trusted friends and adults.
- Read your script aloud so you can note any problems.
- Divide the revision process into several stages.
- Check for grammar and spelling last.

slowly or too quickly. It will also help you notice when stage directions are missing.

Some experts advise rewriting several times, each revision focusing on one specific aspect of your script. These revisions include a rewrite to make sure your script is understandable; a rewrite for structure, plot, and scenes; a rewrite for characters; and a rewrite for dialogue. The final element of revising is polishing the script. This consists of checking for correct grammar and spelling.

Reading aloud helps the writer hear how the script will be performed.

Write for Performance

Sometimes writers need to revise while the play is being staged and rehearsed. An actor may stumble over your words. You may then need to change them. An actor might drone on and even make you get bored. You may need to cut some lines. An actor might repeatedly enter from stage left when your script says to enter from stage right. Stage directions may need to reflect the actor's mannerisms. You might notice inconsistencies from scene to scene, like the carton of ice cream is left melting on the table or the neighbor enters from the right in one scene and the left in another. The cost of production may mean cutting scenes and changing settings and props.

As the writer, you may want to hold on to your precious words. But once they go on the stage, they belong to the actors. You must be a team player, committed

Directors may need to change the script to better fit the cast.

to making the script work well for everyone involved.

The list of those who will interpret your work is long: the director, the actors, the scenic designer, the lighting designer, the costume designer, the producer, and the audience. You may also get your share of critics who will want to write about your play's performance. Each of these types of people may have his or her own view of how your play should work. Just remember you all have a common goal: the best performance possible. By the time the final curtain closes, you'll know writing your play was well worth the effort!

Once your script is done, enjoy the performance.

27

Writer's Checklist

✓ Brainstorm ideas for your screenplay or stage play.

✓ Choose a hero and give him or her a goal.

✓ Plan scenes and lay out your plot.

✓ Organize your action into three acts: beginning, middle, and end.

✓ Use scene headings to establish where the action takes place.

✓ Know who the audience is for your play.

✓ Give your hero at least three major challenges of increasing difficulty.

✓ Keep props and change of setting to a minimum.

✓ Put words in your characters' mouths that move the plot forward.

✓ Give your characters activities to carry out on stage.

✓ Revise your script to deal with problems you see.

✓ Revise your script to deal with problems others see.

Glossary

close-up shot
A camera shot taken at close range.

dialogue
A conversation between two or more characters.

director
The person who tells the actors and crew what to do according to the script.

inner conflict
A struggle inside a character's mind.

long shot
A camera shot taken from a distance, allowing a broad view of the scene.

medium shot
A camera shot taken at medium distance, allowing some background to come into view.

outer conflict
A struggle between characters or between characters and outside elements, such as weather.

plot
The main story of a stage play or screenplay.

producer
The person financially responsible for the stage or film production.

scene
A unit of action within a script that has a beginning, a middle, and an end.

scene heading
A short description of where the scene takes place.

villain
The character who opposes the hero and complicates the hero's journey.

For More Information

Books

Guillain, Charlotte. *Writing & Staging Real-Life Plays*. Chicago: Heinemann Raintree, 2016.

Loewen, Nancy. *Action! Writing Your Own Play*. Mankato, MN: Cherry Lake Publishing, 2011.

Miles, Liz. *Writing a Screenplay*. Chicago: Heinemann Raintree, 2010.

Visit 12StoryLibrary.com

Scan the code or use your school's login at **12StoryLibrary.com** for recent updates about this topic and a full digital version of this book. Enjoy free access to:

- Digital ebook
- Breaking news updates
- Live content feeds
- Videos, interactive maps, and graphics
- Additional web resources

Note to educators: Visit 12StoryLibrary.com/register to sign up for free premium website access. Enjoy live content plus a full digital version of every 12-Story Library book you own for every student at your school.

Index

About the Author

Barbara Krasner is the author of many books for children. She teaches creative writing in New Jersey.